THE ELEPHANT MAN

A hundred years ago, the world was very different. Poor people lived in cold, dark homes, and never saw a doctor when they were ill. And if you were poor and very, very ugly ...

This is the story of a poor, ugly man. Nobody loved him, everyone laughed at him. They put him in a cage, like an animal at the zoo. Then one day a doctor saw him and thought, 'This poor man is interesting. I want to study him.' Slowly, the Elephant Man became famous, and everyone wanted to meet him. Even the Queen visited him!

But what was the Elephant Man really like? Did he think and feel like other people? Was he a sad, angry man? Could he ever smile and laugh, and forget his ugly face and his strange, ugly body?

OXFORD BOOKWORMS LIBRARY
True Stories

The Elephant Man

Stage 1 (400 headwords)

Series Editor: Jennifer Bassett
Founder Editor: Tricia Hedge
Activities Editors: Jennifer Bassett and Alison Baxter

TIM VICARY

The Elephant Man

OXFORD UNIVERSITY PRESS

OXFORD

UNIVERSITY PRESS

Great Clarendon Street, Oxford OX2 6DP

Oxford University Press is a department of the University of Oxford.
It furthers the University's objective of excellence in research, scholarship,
and education by publishing worldwide in

Oxford New York

Auckland Cape Town Dar es Salaam Hong Kong Karachi
Kuala Lumpur Madrid Melbourne Mexico City Nairobi
New Delhi Shanghai Taipei Toronto

With offices in

Argentina Austria Brazil Chile Czech Republic France Greece
Guatemala Hungary Italy Japan Poland Portugal Singapore
South Korea Switzerland Thailand Turkey Ukraine Vietnam

OXFORD and OXFORD ENGLISH are registered trade marks of
Oxford University Press in the UK and in certain other countries

ISBN 978 0 19 478904 2

A complete recording of this Bookworms edition of
The Elephant Man is available on audio CD ISBN 978 0 19 478839 7

Printed in China

Illustrated by: Nick Harris

Word count/

CONTENTS

Chapter 1

THE CREATURE IN THE SHOP

My name is Dr Frederick Treves. I am a doctor at the London Hospital. One day in 1884, I saw a picture in the window of a shop near the hospital. I stopped in front of the shop and looked at the picture. At first I felt interested, then I felt angry, then afraid. It was a horrible, ugly picture. There was a man in the picture,

One day, Dr Treves saw a picture in a shop near the hospital.

1

but he did not look like you and me. He did not look like a man. He looked like an elephant.

I read the writing under the picture. It said:

Come in and see the Elephant Man. Two pence.

I opened the door and went in.

There was a man in the shop. He was a dirty man in an old coat with a cigarette in his mouth. 'What do you want?' he asked.

'I'd like to see the elephant man, please,' I said.

The man looked at me angrily. 'Well, you can't,' he said. 'The shop's closing now. You can come back tomorrow.'

'I'm sorry,' I said. 'But I would like to see him now. I have no time tomorrow – I have a lot of work to do. But I can give you more than two pence.'

The man looked at me carefully. Then he took the cigarette out of his mouth and smiled with his yellow teeth.

'All right, sir,' he said. 'Give me twelve pence then.'

I gave him the money and he opened a door at the back of the shop. We went into a little room. The room was cold and dark, and there was a horrible smell in it.

A creature sat on a chair behind a table. I say a creature, because it was not a man or a woman, like you or me. The creature did not move or look at us. It sat very quietly on the chair in the cold, dark, dirty room, and looked at the table. The creature had a cloth over its head, because of the cold. On the table in front of it, there was a dead flower.

'Stand up!' said the shopkeeper, loudly.

The creature stood up slowly. It took the old cloth off its head, and put it on the chair.

It sat very quietly on the chair in the cold, dark, dirty room.

I looked at the creature and felt sad. I am a doctor, so I know a lot about accidents and ill people. I see horrible, ugly things every day. But this creature, this thing, was the worst of all. There were no men or women in the hospital like him.

He wore some old trousers, but no shirt, coat, or shoes, so I could see his body very well. His head was the most interesting thing. It was very, very big – like an enormous bag with a lot of books in it. The head did not have much hair, and there was another bag of brown, dirty skin at the back of it. This skin came down below his neck. I could not see one of his eyes very well, because a lot of skin came down in front of his face, too.

An enormous red tooth came out of his mouth, under his nose. It looked like an elephant's tooth. The mouth and nose were like holes in the face. The face could not smile or laugh or look angry or sad, because the skin could not move. It was dead, like an elephant's face.

There were more bags of dirty skin on the front and back of the creature's body. These bags came down to his legs. The right arm was enormous, and there were bags of skin on it, too. The right hand was like a man's foot.

But the left hand – the left arm and the left hand

were beautiful! The left arm had wonderful skin, and the fingers of the left hand were long and beautiful. It was like a young woman's hand!

'Walk, Merrick!' said the shopkeeper angrily. 'Come on, quickly, move!' He hit the creature with his hand.

Slowly, the creature walked across the room. But he could not walk well. His legs were very big and fat, and he had a bad back. He could not walk far without a stick.

'All right, thank you,' I said. 'Let him sit down. I don't want to see any more.' I felt ill, and the smell in the room was very bad.

'Yes, sir,' said the shopkeeper. 'Sit down, Merrick.'

The left hand was like a woman's hand; the fingers were long and beautiful.

We went out of the room and closed the door. The shopkeeper smiled at me with his yellow teeth.

'Wonderful, sir, isn't it?' he said. 'The best Elephant Man in England! Hundreds of people come to see him, you know, hundreds! I take him all over the country, I do!'

'Yes, very interesting,' I said. 'Can I sit down?'

'Yes, sir, of course. Here's a chair.' He looked at me, smiling. 'Would you like a glass of water, sir?'

'Yes, please,' I said. Then I looked at the things in the dirty shop. There were two or three bad apples and some old black bananas: that was all. 'Er, no ... no, thank you. I'm all right,' I said. 'Did you ... did you call the creature Merrick?'

'That's right, sir. Joseph Merrick. The best Elephant Man in England! I take him all over the country, you know. Lots of people want to see him.'

'Yes, I see. Do you get a lot of money?'

'Well, sometimes we do, sir, yes. But it's difficult, you see, sir, because of the police. The police don't like us, you see, sir. So we can't stay in a town very long. We usually move every week.'

'Yes, I see. Well, anyway, Mr ... er?'

'Silcock, sir. Simon Silcock.'

'Yes, well, Mr Silcock, I'm a doctor at the London Hospital. My name is Dr Treves. I think this ... er ...

Then I looked at the things in the dirty shop.

this man Joseph Merrick is very interesting, and I would like to see him at the hospital. I want to look at him more carefully, you see.'

'Yes sir, I see. But how can he get to the hospital? It's going to be difficult.'

'Why, man? The hospital's not far from here.'

'Well, yes, sir. I know. But, you see, Merrick can't walk very well. He needs help.'

'You can come with him. Do you want more money? Is that it?'

'Well, yes, sir, I do. But, you see, people are afraid of him too … In the road, little boys always run after him

7

and hit him. Then the police get angry because people are afraid. Sometimes they take us to prison.'

'I see,' I said. 'Well, how can he come to the hospital, then?'

'Bring a cab, sir,' said Silcock. 'You can take him to the hospital in a cab.'

Chapter 2
THE CARD

So next day, at seven o'clock, I came to the shop in a cab. There were not very many people in the road, because it was early in the morning. In November it is dark at seven o'clock in the morning, and I could not see the shop very well. I waited five minutes. A postman walked past. Then the door of the shop opened, and the creature, Merrick, came out.

I could not see his face or his body. He had an enormous black hat on his head, like a big box. A grey cloth came down from the hat, in front of his face. There was a hole in the cloth in front of his eyes. He could see out of the hole but I could not see in. He wore a long black coat, too. The coat began at his neck, and ended at his feet, so I could not see his arms, his body, or his legs. On his feet he wore big shoes, like old bags.

He had a stick in his left hand, and he walked very slowly. I opened the door of the cab, and got out.

'Good morning, Mr Merrick,' I said. 'Can you get in?'

'Elpmyupasteps,' he said.

'I'm sorry,' I said. 'I don't understand.'

For a minute he stood by the door of the cab and said nothing. Then he hit the cab with his stick.

'STEPS!' he said loudly. 'Help me up the steps!'

'Help me up the steps!'

Then I understood. There were three steps up into the cab, and he could not get up them.

'Yes, I see. I'm sorry,' I said. 'Let me help you.'

I took his left hand and began to help him. My right hand was behind his back. I felt very strange. His left hand was like a young woman's, but his back, under the coat, was horrible. I could feel the bags of old skin on his back under the coat.

He put one enormous foot on the first step, and then he stopped. After a minute, he moved his second foot slowly. Then he stopped and waited again.

'Hello, sir. Can I help you?'

I looked behind me. It was the postman. And behind him, I could see three young boys. One of the boys laughed.

The postman smiled. 'Is the gentleman ill?' he asked.

I thought quickly. 'Yes. But this is a lady, not a gentleman. I'm a doctor, and she's ill. Take her hand, so I can help her better.'

The postman took Merrick's left hand, and I helped him with two hands from behind. Slowly, very slowly, Merrick went up the steps and into the cab.

One boy was very near the cab. He called to his friends.

'Come and see this, boys! A fat lady in a black coat! And look at that enormous hat!'

The boys laughed. They were very near the cab too, now. I closed the door quickly.

'Thank you,' I said to the postman.

'That's all right, sir,' he said. 'She's a strange lady, sir, isn't she?'

'She's ill, that's all,' I said quickly. 'We're going to the hospital. Goodbye, and thank you.'

The cab drove down the road to the hospital. I looked at Merrick. 'That was difficult, wasn't it?' I said.

'Here is my card.'

At first he said nothing, but then he spoke. His voice was very strange, but I listened to him carefully, and I could understand him.

'The steps were very difficult,' he said. 'But most things are difficult for me.'

'Yes,' I said. 'Nothing is easy for you, is it?'

'No,' he said. He was very quiet for a minute. Then he said, 'Who are you, sir?'

'Who am I? Oh, I'm sorry. My name is Dr Treves. Here, this is my card.'

I gave him a card with my name on. Then I thought, 'That was no good. This man can't read.' But Merrick took the card and looked at it very carefully. Then he put it in his trousers pocket.

I did not talk to him very much at the hospital. I looked at his head and arms and legs and body very carefully. Then I wrote the important things about him in a little book. A nurse helped me. Merrick looked at her sometimes, but she did not smile at him or talk to him. I think she was afraid of him. I think Merrick was afraid too, because he was very quiet.

At four o'clock I took him back to the shop in a cab. The next day I looked in the shop window again, but the picture was not there.

Chapter 3
A LETTER TO 'THE TIMES'

I did not see Merrick again for two years. Then, one day, the police found him. He had my card in his hand, so they brought him to the London Hospital. He was very tired, hungry, and dirty, so I put him to bed in a quiet little room. But he could not stay at the hospital. He was not ill, and of course the beds in the hospital are for ill people. We have no beds for hungry people, or ugly people.

One day the police brought Merrick to the hospital.

I told the Hospital Chairman, Mr Carr Gomm, about Merrick. He listened carefully, and then he wrote a letter to the editor of *The Times* newspaper.

From The Times, *December 4th, 1886*
A Letter to the Editor

Dear Sir,

I am writing to you about a man in our hospital. He needs your help. His name is Joseph Merrick, and he is 27 years old. He is not ill, but he cannot go out of the hospital because he is very, very ugly. Nobody likes to look at him, and some people are afraid of him. We call him the 'Elephant Man'.

Two years ago, Merrick lived in a shop near the London Hospital. For two pence, people could see him and laugh at him. One day Dr Frederick Treves – a hospital doctor – saw Merrick, brought him to this hospital, and looked at him carefully. Dr Treves could not help Merrick, but he gave him his card.

Then the shopkeeper, Silcock, took Merrick to Belgium. A lot of people in Belgium wanted to see him, and so after a year Merrick had £50. But then Silcock took Merrick's £50, left Merrick in Belgium, and went back to London.

Merrick came back to London by himself. Everyone on the train and the ship looked at him, and laughed at him. In London, the police put him in prison. But then they saw Dr Treves's card, and brought Merrick to the London Hospital.

This man has no money, and he cannot work. His face and body are very, very ugly, so of course many people are afraid of him. But he is a very interesting man. He can read and write, and he thinks a lot. He is a good, quiet man. Sometimes he makes things with his hands and gives them to the nurses, because they are kind to him.

He remembers his mother, and he has a picture of her. She was beautiful and kind, he says. But he never sees her now. She gave him to Silcock a long time ago.

Can the readers of *The Times* help us? This man is not ill, but he needs a home. We can give him a room at the hospital, but we need some money. Please write to me at the London Hospital.

Yours faithfully,

F.C. Carr Gomm
Chairman of the London Hospital

*Sometimes he makes things with his hands
and gives them to the nurses.*

The readers of *The Times* are very kind people. They gave us a lot of money. After one week, we had £50,000, so Merrick could live in the hospital for all his life. We could give him a home.

Chapter 4

MERRICK'S FIRST HOME

We gave Merrick two rooms at the back of the hospital. One room was a bathroom, so he could have a bath every day. Soon his skin was much better, and there was no horrible smell.

The second room had a bed, table, and chairs. I visited him every day, and talked to him. He loved reading, and talking about books. At first he did not know many books: the Bible, and one or two newspapers, that's all. But I gave him some books of love stories, and he liked them very much. He read them again and again, and talked about them often. For him, the men and women in these books were alive, like you and me. He was very happy.

But sometimes it was difficult for him. At first, one or two people in the hospital laughed at Merrick because he was ugly. Sometimes, they brought their friends to look at him. One day a new nurse came to the hospital, and nobody told her about Merrick. She

We gave Merrick two rooms at the back of the hospital.

I was very angry with the nurse.

took his food to his room, and opened the door. Then she saw him. She screamed, dropped the food on the floor, and ran out of the room.

I was very angry with the nurse, and went to see Merrick. He was not happy about it, but he was not very angry. I think he felt sorry for the girl.

'People don't like looking at me. I know that, Dr Treves,' he said. 'They usually laugh or scream.'

'Well, I don't want nurses to laugh at you, Joseph,' I said angrily. 'I want them to help you.'

'Thank you, doctor,' he said, in his strange slow voice. 'But it's not important. Everyone laughs at me. I understand that.'

I looked at him sadly. In his one good hand, his left

hand, he had the little picture of his mother. He looked at the picture for a minute, and then put it by a flower on the table. A tear ran out of his eye and down the skin of his enormous, ugly face.

'Dr Treves,' he said, slowly. 'You and the nurses are very kind, and I'm very happy here. Thank you very much. But … I know I can't stay here long, and … I would like to live in a lighthouse, after the hospital, please. A lighthouse, or a home for blind people. I think those are the best places for me.'

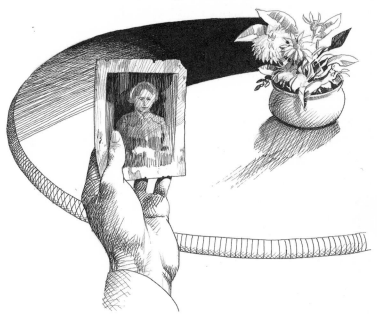

In his one good hand he had the picture of his mother.

'What do you mean?' I asked. 'Why?'

He did not look at me. He put the flower on the picture and looked at it carefully.

'Lighthouses have sea all round them, don't they?' he said. 'Nobody could look at me in a lighthouse, so I would be happy there. And blind people can see nothing, so they couldn't see me, could they?'

'But Joseph,' I said, 'this is your home. You live here now. You aren't going to leave the hospital.'

'Not today, perhaps,' he said. 'But soon. You are a kind man, Dr Treves. But I can't stay here very long. I have no money.'

I smiled. 'Joseph,' I said. 'This is your *home* now. Don't you understand? You can stay here all your life.' Very carefully, I told him about the letter to *The Times*, and the money.

I don't think he understood at first, so I told him again. He was very quiet for a minute. Then he stood up, and walked up and down the room very quickly. A strange sound came from him, like laughing.

*A beautiful young woman came to the hospital
and shook Merrick's hand.*

Chapter 5

AN IMPORTANT VISITOR

I did not want Merrick to live by himself, like a man in a lighthouse. He read his books, and talked to me, but I wanted him to talk to more people. And I wanted him to talk to women.

Merrick read about women in his books, but he did not often talk to women. He met the nurses every day, but they did not talk to him very much. For them, he was always a creature, not a man.

One day, one of my friends, a beautiful young woman, came to the hospital. I told her about Merrick, and took her to his room. She opened the door, and smiled at him.

'Good morning, Mr Merrick,' she said. Then she shook his hand.

Merrick looked at her for a minute with his mouth open. Then he sat down on his bed, with his head in his hand, and cried. He cried for nearly five minutes. The tears ran down his face, between his fingers, and onto the floor.

My friend sat on the bed beside him and put her hand on his arm. She said nothing, but she smiled at

For the first time in his life, Merrick had some friends.

him and shook his hand again before she left.

'Dr Treves,' he said to me that night. 'That lady was wonderful! My mother smiled at me once, many years ago, but no women smile at me now. But this lady smiled at me too, and she shook my hand! A beautiful lady smiled at me and shook my hand!'

My young lady friend came again the next week, and talked to Merrick for half an hour. The week after that, she came again with a friend. They gave him some books, and had a cup of tea with him. It was wonderful for him. For the first time in his life, he had some friends. He was a very happy man. He sat in his room, and read his books, and said no more about living on a lighthouse.

*'Joseph, this is Her Majesty Queen Alexandra,
the Queen of England.'*

People began to read about Merrick in the
newspapers, so he had a lot of visitors. Everybody
wanted to see him. A lot of important ladies and
gentlemen visited him. They smiled at him, shook his
hand, and gave him books. Merrick liked talking to
these people, and he began to forget about his ugly
body. His visitors never laughed at him. He began to
feel like a man, not a creature.

One wonderful day, a very important lady came to
the hospital to visit him. I met the lady, and took her to
his room. Then I opened the door, and smiled at him.

'Good morning, Joseph,' I said. 'There is a new
visitor to see you today. A very famous lady.'

Merrick stood up beside his table. He did not smile, because his face could not smile, but his eyes looked happy.

'That's good,' he said. 'Who is it?'

I moved away from the door, and the visitor walked in. 'Your Majesty, this is Joseph Merrick,' I said. 'Joseph, this is Her Majesty, Queen Alexandra, the Queen of England.'

Queen Alexandra smiled at him. 'How do you do, Mr Merrick,' she said. 'I'm very pleased to meet you.' Then she shook his hand.

Merrick did not move. For nearly half a minute he stood and looked at her with his mouth open. Then he spoke, in his strange, slow voice.

'How … how do you do, Your Majesty,' he said. But I don't think the Queen understood him, because he tried to get down on his knees at the same time. It was very difficult for him, because of his enormous legs.

'No, please, Mr Merrick, do get up,' said the Queen. 'I would like to talk to you. Can we sit at your table?'

'Yes … yes, of course,' he said. They sat at the table. She took his left hand, the good hand, in hers. She looked at the hand carefully, and then smiled at Merrick again.

'I often read about you in the newspapers,' she said.

'You are a very interesting man, Mr Merrick. You have a very difficult life, but people say you're happy. Is it true? Are you happy now?'

'Oh, yes, Your Majesty, yes!' said Merrick. 'I'm a very happy man! I have a home here now, and friends, and my books. I'm happy every hour of the day!'

'What a wonderful story!' she said. 'I'm very pleased to hear it. Now, tell me about your reading. I see you have a lot of books here.'

'Oh, yes, Your Majesty. I love my books,' said Merrick. And for nearly half an hour they sat and talked about books. The Queen gave him a little book, and some red flowers, before she left.

After her visit, Merrick began to sing. He could not

sing easily, of course, because of his mouth, but all that day there was a strange, happy noise in his room. He looked at the flowers carefully, and put them on his table.

He had many visits from the Queen, and at Christmas she sent him a Christmas card.

Windsor Castle
20th December 1888

Dear Joseph,

Here is a small Christmas present for you. I think it looks like me, doesn't it? I do like visiting you very much, and I am going to come to the hospital again in the New Year.

Happy Christmas!

Your friend,

Alexandra.

The present was a picture of Queen Alexandra, with her name on it. Merrick cried over it, and put it carefully by the bed in his room. Then he sat down and wrote a letter to the Queen. It was the first letter of his life.

The London Hospital
23rd December 1888

My dear Queen,

Thank you very, very much for your wonderful card and the beautiful picture. It is the best thing in my room, the very best, the most beautiful thing I have. This is the first Christmas in my life, and my first Christmas present. Perhaps I had a Christmas with my mother once, but I do not remember it. I have my mother's picture too, and she is beautiful, like you. But now I know many famous ladies and kind people like Dr Treves, and I am a very happy man. I am happy too because I am going to see you in the New Year.

Happy Christmas to you, my dear friend.

With all my love,
Joseph Merrick

Chapter 6

OUTSIDE THE HOSPITAL

Merrick had a lot of friends now, but he was more like a child than a man. He could read about things, and talk to his visitors, but he could not go out of the hospital by himself. He thought and played like a child.

After Christmas, he wanted to go to the theatre. This was very difficult, because I did not want the people in the theatre to see him. But a kind lady from the theatre – Mrs Kendal – helped us. We bought tickets for a box at the side of the theatre. We went to the theatre in a cab with dark windows, and we went into the theatre by a door at the back – the Queen's door. Nobody saw us.

Three nurses sat at the front of the box, and Merrick and I sat in the dark behind them. Nobody in the theatre could see us, but we could see the play.

It was a children's Christmas play. Merrick loved it. It was a most wonderful, exciting story. Often he laughed, and sometimes he tried to sing like the children in the theatre. He was like a child. For him, everything in the story was true.

Once he was very afraid, because the bad man in the play was angry and had a knife. At first Merrick

We bought tickets for a box at the side of the theatre.

wanted to leave the theatre, but I stopped him. Then he
was very angry with this bad man in the play. He hit his
hand on his chair, and stood up and talked to the man.
But nobody heard him. When the bad man went to
prison, Merrick laughed.

Merrick thought the beautiful young lady in the play
was wonderful. He wanted to talk to her too. At the
end of the play he was very happy because she married
a good young man.

He remembered this play for a long time, and he
talked a lot about the people in it. 'What do you think
they did after we left?' he asked me. 'Where do the
young lady and the young man live? What are they
doing now?'

'I don't know,' I said. 'Perhaps they live in the country.'

Merrick thought about this for a long time. Then he said: 'Dr Treves, can I go to the country, please? I saw the country once from a train, but I never went there. I often read about it in books. It's very beautiful, isn't it? I would like to see it.'

The visit to the theatre was difficult but a visit to the country was more difficult. But again, one of his new friends helped us. She had a small house in the country, and Merrick could stay in it for the summer, she said.

I took Merrick to the country in a train with dark windows, so nobody could see him. Then we went in a cab to the country house.

There were a lot of trees near the house, but no people lived near it. A countryman brought food to the house every day, but no people came near it.

I stayed with him that night. At night, it was very dark and quiet. In the morning, hundreds of birds sang in the trees, and everything outside the house was green. Merrick walked under the big trees, looking at things happily, and singing his strange song.

I went back to London, but Merrick stayed there for six weeks. He was wonderfully happy. Every week, he wrote me a letter.

Apple Tree House,
West Wickham,
Berkshire.
21st July 1889

Dear Dr Treves,

I had a wonderful day again today. It was very warm, so I walked under the trees and sat by a stream.

No people lived near the house in the country.

A lot of birds are my friends now.

The water in the stream made a beautiful noise, like singing. Did you know that? I listened to it for two hours.

Lots of little birds came near me. One had a red body in front, and a brown back. I gave it some bread, and it sat on my hand. A lot of birds are my friends, now.

I watched the fish in the stream, too. They were very exciting, because they move very fast. One minute they were there, and the next minute I couldn't see them. But I waited quietly, and they always came back. I put my hand in the water, but I couldn't touch them.

I met a big dog yesterday. It made a very loud noise, but I was not afraid. I sat down quietly and looked at it, and it came and smelt my hand. I saw it again today, and gave it some bread. It likes me now.

I am going to put some flowers from the country in this letter. There are hundreds of flowers here. Did you know that? I like the little blue ones best, but they are all beautiful. I have lots of them in my room. I give them water every morning. Little flowers are very thirsty, you know!

I am very happy here, doctor, but I want to see you again soon, too.

With love from your friend,
Joseph Merrick

At the end of the summer he came back to London. He was very well, and his skin looked much better. He talked about the country a lot, but he was happy to see his friends and his books again, too.

Chapter 7

THE LAST LETTER

Six months later, in April 1890, I found him dead in bed. He was on his back in bed, so at first I thought he was asleep. I talked to him, but he did not move. Then I saw that the skin on his face was blue, so I knew he was dead.

*He could only sleep with his arms around his legs,
and his head on his knees.*

He did not usually sleep on his back. His enormous head was very heavy, so he usually sat up in bed with his arms round his legs, and his head on his knees. He could sleep well like this.

But he wanted to sleep on his back like you and me. He tried to sleep on his back that night, but his heavy head came off the bed, and he broke his neck. He died very quickly.

Next day, the Chairman of the London Hospital, Mr Carr Gomm, wrote to the editor of *The Times* again.

I found him dead in bed.

The Times, April 16th, 1890

Dear Sir,

Three and a half years ago I wrote to you about a man called Joseph Merrick. This man was called the 'Elephant Man' because he was born with a very ugly body. Merrick was not ill, but he could not work, and he had no money.

The readers of *The Times* felt sorry for him, and they gave me a lot of money for Merrick. Because of this money, we could give Merrick a home in the London Hospital. It was his first good home, and for three and a half years he lived here happily. The doctors and nurses of the hospital helped him, and many important people visited him. He read many books, he went to the theatre, and in the summer he stayed in the country for six weeks. Because of your readers' money, we could give him a happy life.

Last night Joseph Merrick died quietly in his bed. He was a man with a very ugly body, but he was a good, kind man, and he had a lot of friends. We liked to talk to him, and we are all very sorry because he is dead. A lot of people are going to remember him for a long time.

There is some money left, so I am going to give it to the hospital. Thank you, sir, for your help.

Yours faithfully,
F.C. Carr Gomm
Chairman of the London Hospital

GLOSSARY

bath when you want to wash all your body, you sit in a bath full of water

below under

beside next to

Bible the most important book for Christians

box (in a theatre) a small 'room'; you can watch the stage from a box, but other people can't see you

cab an old word for 'taxi'

card a piece of paper with your name and address on it (a visiting card); or a card with a picture and a greeting on it (e.g. a Christmas card)

chairman an important man in the hospital

cloth trousers, coats, dresses, etc. are made from cloth

country (the) not the town

creature a living animal

drop *(v)* to let something fall

editor the most important person in a newspaper office

elephant a very big grey animal with a long nose and big ears

enormous very big

faithfully (Yours faithfully) you write 'Yours faithfully' at the end of a formal letter

fingers you have five fingers on each hand

fish fish live in rivers and in the sea

food what you eat

gentleman a man from an important family

glass *(n)* you drink tea from a cup; you drink water from a glass

heavy it is difficult to carry heavy things; 1,000 kilos is very
heavy

himself (by himself) nobody was with him

hip the place where your leg joins your body

hole an empty space or opening in something

horrible not nice; people are often afraid of 'horrible' things

kind nice, good; a kind person often helps people

knee the middle of your leg where it bends

lady a woman from an important family

life your life stops when you die

lighthouse a tall building by or in the sea, with a strong light;
the light tells ships that there are dangerous rocks

like *(prep)* not different: a river is like the sea, because it is
made of water

loudly with a lot of noise

Majesty (Her/His/Your) when you speak to a queen or a king,
you say 'Your Majesty'

marry to take somebody as your husband or wife

mirror a piece of special glass; you can see your face in a mirror

neck your neck is between your head and your body

newspaper you read a newspaper to know what is happening in
the world

nose your nose is between your eyes and your mouth

place where something or someone is (a room, a house, a town,
etc.)

play *(n)* you go to the theatre to see a play

police the police help people; they also put bad people in prison

present something that you give to or get from somebody (e.g.
a birthday present)

prison a building for bad people; they must stay there and
cannot leave

Queen (the) the most important woman in Britain

sad not happy

scream *(v)* to make a loud high cry because you are afraid or angry

shake hands (past tense **shook**) to hold somebody's hand and move it up and down as a greeting

shopkeeper a person who has a small shop

side the part of something that is not the top, bottom, front or back

skin you have skin all over your body; people have different skin colours

smell (past tense **smelt**) you see with your eyes; you smell with your nose

step a place to put your foot when you go up or down

stick *(n)* a long piece of wood; Merrick walks with a stick

strange different

stream a small river

tears water from your eyes when you cry

theatre a building where you go to see plays

touch *(v)* to feel something with your hand

ugly not beautiful

voice you talk with your voice

The Elephant Man

ACTIVITIES

Before Reading

1 Read the story introduction on the first page of the book, and the back cover. How much do you know now about the Elephant Man?
Tick one box for each sentence.

		YES	NO
1	People laugh at him.	☐	☐
2	He is very old.	☐	☐
3	His mother loves him.	☐	☐
4	People put him in a cage, like an animal.	☐	☐
5	Children like him.	☐	☐
6	A doctor wants to study him.	☐	☐
7	His name is Joseph Merrick.	☐	☐

2 What is going to happen in the story? Can you guess? Tick one box for each sentence.

		YES	NO	PERHAPS
1	The doctor helps the Elephant Man.	☐	☐	☐
2	The Elephant Man kills somebody.	☐	☐	☐
3	The Elephant Man lives to be a very old man.	☐	☐	☐
4	The Elephant Man finds a home.	☐	☐	☐
5	The Elephant Man finds a wife.	☐	☐	☐
6	The Elephant Man makes some friends.	☐	☐	☐
7	Somebody kills the Elephant Man.	☐	☐	☐

While Reading

Read Chapters 1 and 2, and answer these questions.

1 What did Dr Treves see in the window of the shop?
2 Who did Dr Treves give twelve pence to?
3 How did Dr Treves feel when he saw the Elephant Man?
4 Why couldn't the Elephant Man walk well?
5 How did Dr Treves and Merrick get to the hospital?
6 What did Dr Treves give Merrick?

Dr Treves wrote about Merrick in a little book. Use these words to complete his sentences. (Use each word once.) Then draw a picture of the Elephant Man.

bag, big, enormous, fingers, hair, man's, nose, skin, tooth

1 His head is very _____, and it looks like an enormous
    _____ with a lot of books in it.
2 There is not much _____ on his head, and the _____ on
    his face cannot move.
3 An enormous red _____ comes out of his mouth, under
    his _____.
4 The right arm is _____ and the right hand is like a _____
    foot, but the _____ of the left hand are long and
    beautiful.

Read Chapters 3 and 4. Choose the best question-word for these questions, and then answer them.

Why / Who / What

1 … did the police bring Merrick to the hospital?
2 … did Mr Carr Gomm write to *The Times* newspaper?
3 … did the readers of *The Times* do?
4 … did Merrick have a picture of?
5 … did the nurse do when she saw Merrick?
6 … did Merrick want to live in a lighthouse?

When the police found Merrick (in Chapter 3), they asked him some questions. Complete their conversation. (Use as many words as you like.)

POLICE: Now, Mr Merrick. Where do you live, sir?

MERRICK: _____

POLICE: Do you have any money, sir?

MERRICK: _____

POLICE: Why not? What happened to your money?

MERRICK: _____

POLICE: You can't stay in prison. Where do you want to go now?

MERRICK: _____

POLICE: Why? Do you know somebody there?

MERRICK: _____

POLICE: Ah, I see. All right, sir. Let's go and see him now.

Before you read Chapters 5, 6, and 7, think about Merrick's life. Is it going to be different now? Some of these things are going to happen. Can you guess which?

He never goes out.	He visits a lighthouse.
He reads a lot.	He goes to a theatre.
His mother visits him.	A nurse wants to marry him.
The Queen visits him.	He is very happy.
He makes new friends.	He gets very ill.

Read Chapter 5. Who said or wrote this, and to whom?

1 'A beautiful lady smiled at me and shook my hand!'
2 'There is a new visitor to see you today.'
3 'I often read about you in the newspapers.'
4 'I'm happy every hour of the day!'
5 'I do like visiting you very much.'
6 'It is the best thing in my room, the very best …'

Read Chapters 6 and 7. Here are some untrue sentences about them. Change them into true sentences.

1 Merrick often went out of the hospital by himself.
2 Merrick thought and played like a man.
3 Merrick was very pleased with the bad man in the play.
4 Merrick did not like staying in the country.
5 Merrick usually slept on his back.
6 Nobody was sorry when the Elephant Man died.

After Reading

1 Can you find the eleven words from the story hidden in this word search? Words go from left to right, and from top to bottom.

N	V	F	I	S	H	K	W	D	P
U	F	L	O	D	O	C	T	O	R
R	G	H	D	T	S	D	K	G	L
S	D	C	Y	D	P	E	U	R	F
E	V	O	J	F	I	N	G	E	R
S	Q	U	H	K	T	E	L	R	I
S	Z	N	W	R	A	G	Y	P	E
W	V	T	G	G	L	M	T	F	N
B	I	R	D	S	H	M	K	Y	D
Q	E	Y	J	Q	U	E	E	N	S

Now use ten of the words from the word search to complete this passage.

Joseph Merrick, the Elephant Man, lived in the London
_____. He was a very _____ man but most of the _____
liked him. _____ Alexandra was one of his _____. One
summer he stayed in a house in the _____. He saw _____
in a stream, and talked to _____ and a _____. 'He was very
happy there,' _____ Treves said.

2 Here is a conversation between Dr Treves and the new nurse (see pages 17 and 18). The conversation is in the wrong order. Write it out in the correct order and put in the speakers' names. The nurse speaks first (number 2).

1 _____ 'Yes. I started work this morning.'

2 _____ 'Dr Treves, Dr Treves! Help!'

3 _____ 'I dropped his food on the floor and ran out. I was afraid. Is he very ill?'

4 _____ 'Oh, doctor, there's a horrible creature in Mr Merrick's room!'

5 _____ 'What's the matter, nurse? Why are you screaming?'

6 _____ 'All right, doctor. Thank you.'

7 _____ 'That's Mr Merrick, nurse! He looks like that. What did you do in the room?'

8 _____ 'It's got an enormous head with an elephant's tooth in its mouth, and a big horrible arm!'

9 _____ 'No, Mr Merrick isn't ill, but he's very ugly. Now sit down and listen to me, nurse. Is this your first day here?'

10 _____ 'What does this horrible creature look like?'

11 _____ 'Well, don't be afraid of Mr Merrick. He isn't horrible. He's a nice, kind man. Now go back in that room, and talk to him. All right?'

3 Here is a new illustration for the story. Find the best place
   in the story to put the picture, and answer these questions.

   The picture goes on page _____.

   1 Where is the Elephant Man going in this picture?
   2 Where was he before this?
   3 What happened to him when he arrived?

   Now write a caption for the illustration.

Caption: _____

4 **Here is a newspaper story about the Elephant Man. Use the linking words below to complete the story. (Use some of the words more than once.)**

but / and / because / so / when

Last night Joseph Merrick, the famous 'Elephant Man', died. Merrick did not have an easy life. His mother gave him to a man called Silcock, _____ Silcock took him from town to town, to make money. _____ Silcock left him in Belgium, Merrick came back to England. He was not ill, _____ he could not work, _____ the London Hospital gave him a home. There, people were kind to him for the first time in his life, _____ he had many friends.

'He had a very ugly body,' said his friend Dr Treves, '_____ we all liked him _____ he was a good, kind man.'

5 *The Elephant Man* **is a true story. Which of these sentences do you agree (A) or disagree (D) with? Can you say why?**

1 It is a very sad story.

2 It is a sad story, but a happy one too.

3 Joseph Merrick's mother was a bad woman, because she gave her son to Silcock.

4 Very ugly people, like Joseph Merrick, can never have a happy life.

5 Doctors and hospitals can do wonderful things now, so people like Joseph Merrick don't have unhappy lives.

ABOUT THE AUTHOR

Tim Vicary is an experienced teacher and writer, and has written several stories for the Oxford Bookworms Library. Many of these are in the Thriller & Adventure series, such as *White Death* (at Stage 1) or, like *The Elephant Man*, in the True Stories series, such as *The Coldest Place on Earth* (also at Stage 1), which tells the story of the race between Scott and Amundsen to the South Pole. He has also published two long novels, *The Blood upon the Rose* and *Cat and Mouse*.

Tim Vicary has two children, and keeps dogs, cats, and horses. He lives and works in York, in the north of England.

OXFORD BOOKWORMS LIBRARY

Classics • Crime & Mystery • Factfiles • Fantasy & Horror
Human Interest • Playscripts • Thriller & Adventure
True Stories • World Stories

The OXFORD BOOKWORMS LIBRARY provides enjoyable reading in English, with a wide range of classic and modern fiction, non-fiction, and plays. It includes original and adapted texts in seven carefully graded language stages, which take learners from beginner to advanced level. An overview is given on the next pages.

All Stage 1 titles are available as audio recordings, as well as over eighty other titles from Starter to Stage 6. All Starters and many titles at Stages 1 to 4 are specially recommended for younger learners. Every Bookworm is illustrated, and Starters and Factfiles have full-colour illustrations.

The OXFORD BOOKWORMS LIBRARY also offers extensive support. Each book contains an introduction to the story, notes about the author, a glossary, and activities. Additional resources include tests and worksheets, and answers for these and for the activities in the books. There is advice on running a class library, using audio recordings, and the many ways of using Oxford Bookworms in reading programmes. Resource materials are available on the website <www.oup.com/bookworms>.

The *Oxford Bookworms Collection* is a series for advanced learners. It consists of volumes of short stories by well-known authors, both classic and modern. Texts are not abridged or adapted in any way, but carefully selected to be accessible to the advanced student.

You can find details and a full list of titles in the *Oxford Bookworms Library Catalogue* and *Oxford English Language Teaching Catalogues*, and on the website <www.oup.com/bookworms>.

THE OXFORD BOOKWORMS LIBRARY
GRADING AND SAMPLE EXTRACTS

STARTER • 250 HEADWORDS

present simple – present continuous – imperative –
can/cannot, must – *going to* (future) – simple gerunds …

Her phone is ringing – but where is it?

Sally gets out of bed and looks in her bag. No phone. She looks under the bed. No phone. Then she looks behind the door. There is her phone. Sally picks up her phone and answers it. *Sally's Phone*

STAGE I • 400 HEADWORDS

… past simple – coordination with *and, but, or* –
subordination with *before, after, when, because, so* …

I knew him in Persia. He was a famous builder and I worked with him there. For a time I was his friend, but not for long. When he came to Paris, I came after him – I wanted to watch him. He was a very clever, very dangerous man. *The Phantom of the Opera*

STAGE 2 • 700 HEADWORDS

… present perfect – *will* (future) – *(don't) have to, must not, could* –
comparison of adjectives – simple *if* clauses – past continuous –
tag questions – *ask/tell* + infinitive …

While I was writing these words in my diary, I decided what to do. I must try to escape. I shall try to get down the wall outside. The window is high above the ground, but I have to try. I shall take some of the gold with me – if I escape, perhaps it will be helpful later. *Dracula*

... should, may – present perfect continuous – *used to* – past perfect –
causative – relative clauses – indirect statements ...

Of course, it was most important that no one should see
Colin, Mary, or Dickon entering the secret garden. So Colin
gave orders to the gardeners that they must all keep away
from that part of the garden in future. *The Secret Garden*

... past perfect continuous – passive (simple forms) –
would conditional clauses – indirect questions –
relatives with *where/when* – gerunds after prepositions/phrases ...

I was glad. Now Hyde could not show his face to the world
again. If he did, every honest man in London would be proud
to report him to the police. *Dr Jekyll and Mr Hyde*

... future continuous – future perfect –
passive (modals, continuous forms) –
would have conditional clauses – modals + perfect infinitive ...

If he had spoken Estella's name, I would have hit him. I was so
angry with him, and so depressed about my future, that I could
not eat the breakfast. Instead I went straight to the old house.
Great Expectations

... passive (infinitives, gerunds) – advanced modal meanings –
clauses of concession, condition

When I stepped up to the piano, I was confident. It was as if I
knew that the prodigy side of me really did exist. And when I
started to play, I was so caught up in how lovely I looked that
I didn't worry how I would sound. *The Joy Luck Club*

Ned Kelly: A True Story

CHRISTINE LINDOP

When he was a boy, he was poor and hungry. When he was a young man, he was still poor and still hungry. He learnt how to steal horses, he learnt how to fight, he learnt how to live – outside the law. Australia in the 1870s was a hard, wild place. Rich people had land, poor people didn't. So the rich got richer, and the poor stayed poor.

Some say Ned Kelly was a bad man. Some say he was a good man but the law was bad. This is the true story of Australia's most famous outlaw.

The Omega Files – Short Stories

JENNIFER BASSETT

In EDI (the European Department of Intelligence in Brussels) there are some very secret files – the Omega Files. There are strange, surprising, and sometimes horrible stories in these files, but not many people know about them. You never read about them in the newspapers.

Hawker and Jude know all about the Omega Files, because they work for EDI. They think fast, they move fast, and they learn some very strange things. They go all over the world, asking difficult questions in dangerous places, but they don't always find the answers …